My Life with
Asthma

written by **Mari Schuh** • art by **Ana Sebastián**

AMICUS ILLUSTRATED
is published by Amicus
P.O. Box 227, Mankato, MN 56002
www.amicuspublishing.us

Editor: Rebecca Glaser
Series Designer: Kathleen Petelinsek
Book Designer: Catherine Berthiaume

Library of Congress Cataloging-in-Publication Data
Names: Schuh, Mari C., 1975- author. | Sebastián, Ana, illustrator.
Title: My life with asthma / by Mari C. Schuh ; illustrated by Ana Sebastián.
Description: Mankato, Minnesota : Amicus Illustrated, [2023] | Series: My life with... |
Includes bibliographical references. | Audience: Ages 6-9 | Audience: Grades 2-3 |
Summary: "Meet Tayla! She loves to dance. She also has asthma. Tayla is real and so are her experiences. Learn about
her life in this illustrated narrative nonfiction picture book for elementary students"–Provided by publisher.
Identifiers: LCCN 2022006143 (print) | LCCN 2022006144 (ebook) |
ISBN 9781645494508 (library binding) | ISBN 9781681528571 (paperback) | ISBN 9781645494546 (pdf)
Subjects: LCSH: Asthma–Juvenile literature.
Classification: LCC RC591 .S333 2023 (print) | LCC RC591 (ebook) |
DDC 616.2/38--dc23/eng/20220210
LC record available at https://lccn.loc.gov/2022006143
LC ebook record available at https://lccn.loc.gov/2022006144

For Tayla and her family–MS

About the Author
Mari Schuh's love of reading began with cereal boxes at
the kitchen table. Today she is the author of hundreds of
nonfiction books for beginning readers. With each book, Mari
hopes she's helping kids learn a little bit more about the world
around them. Find out more about her at marischuh.com.

About the Illustrator
Ana Sebastián is an illustrator living in Spain. She studied
Fine Arts at University of Zaragoza and Université Michel de
Montaigne, Bordeaux. Specializing in digital illustration she
completed her education with a master's degree in digital
illustration for concept art and visual development.

Hi! I'm Tayla. Like many kids, I'm often on the move. I love to dance! I have been dancing since I was six years old. I also have asthma. Let me tell you about my life.

Asthma affects the lungs. Airways in the lungs swell up and become narrow. These tubes can make extra mucus, too. It's hard for air to get through. This makes it difficult to breathe.

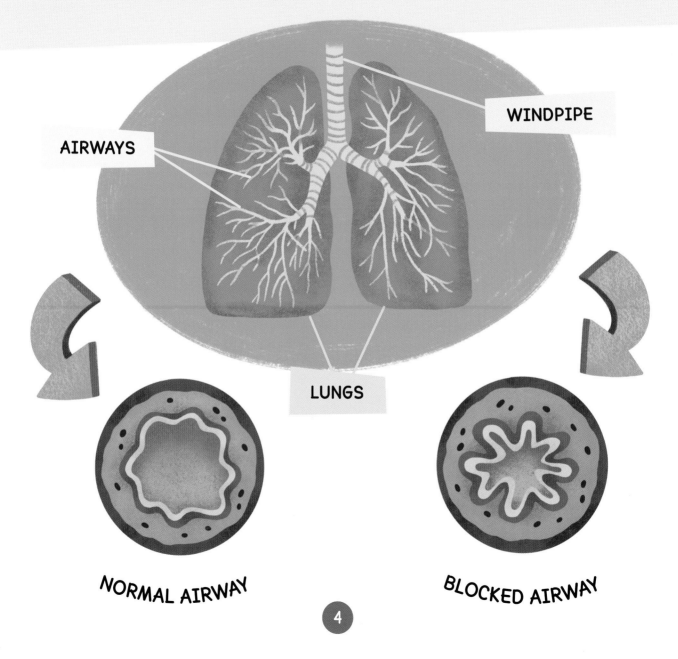

AIRWAYS

WINDPIPE

LUNGS

NORMAL AIRWAY

BLOCKED AIRWAY

People can have asthma attacks, or flare-ups. Asthma attacks are scary. They can be serious. People cough and wheeze. They feel out of breath. Their chest feels tight. Attacks like mine last just a few minutes. Others last for several hours.

Asthma can run in families. My oldest sister has asthma. One of my uncles does, too. Our asthma is mild. We need asthma medicine, but it's not too serious. But for some people, asthma can affect them all the time.

When I was five years old, I got very sick. I had a fever and was really tired. It was hard to breathe. I slept a lot and missed a week of school.

Doctors took X-rays of my lungs. I also breathed into a peak flow meter. It showed how my airways were working. That's when I learned that I had asthma.

Medicine helps me breathe easier. It opens up my airways. I breathe in the medicine using an inhaler. One inhaler controls my asthma. It keeps me from having an attack. I often use it before I exercise. My other inhaler is for emergencies. It quickly ends an asthma attack.

Many things cause asthma attacks. They are called triggers. My triggers include hot weather, dairy products, having a cold, and too much exercise. I take breaks until I feel better. If I have breathing problems at school, I go to the nurse's office. I keep my inhaler there.

People have different triggers. Polluted air and having the flu can give people asthma attacks. My oldest sister and I also have allergies. For us, allergens like pollen and dust are triggers. They can give us asthma attacks.

Strong emotions can cause asthma attacks. During a dance routine, I sometimes get scared during lifts. What if they drop me? My breathing changes, and then I have a mild asthma attack. I face my fears and finish the dance. Then I use my inhaler and drink water.

Sometimes I miss my mom when she's away. I cry and have anxiety. My chest feels tight, like I can't get enough air.

When I have trouble breathing, I panic. I have learned how to calm down. I use my inhaler to breathe easier. Then I take slow, deep breaths. I often pray.

Exercise is good for me. It keeps my lungs strong. I'm on the step team at school. We use our bodies to make sounds and rhythms. We stomp, clap, and speak to make music. It's fun!

I have learned to control my asthma. It does not stop me from being active. Before I exercise, I remember to use my inhaler. Then I'm ready to go. I can do everything I want to do.

Meet Tayla

Hi! I'm Tayla. I live in Baltimore, Maryland, with my family. I have three older sisters and two nephews. My hobbies are dancing, reading, and drawing. I also like to play video games and hang out with my friends. Art is my favorite subject. My favorite food is homemade pasta salad.

Respecting People with Asthma

People with asthma have different triggers. One person might get asthma from exercising too hard. Another person might have an asthma attack in very cold weather.

If you see someone having trouble breathing, tell an adult. Stay calm and ask for help.

Kids with asthma want to have fun, just like other kids. Be sure to invite them to play.

If you know someone with asthma, be a good friend. Remind them to bring their medicine with them.

Kids with asthma might need to take breaks when they play. Be patient and understanding.

Helpful Words

airways   Tubes that carry air to and from the lungs.

allergen   Something that makes a person with an allergy sick. Dust, pollen, pet fur, and certain foods are common allergens.

allergy   A reaction in the body caused by something that is harmless for most people.

anxiety   A strong feeling of worry or fear that may cause changes in the body.

asthma   A breathing illness of the airways.

inhaler   A tool that lets a person breathe in asthma medicine.

mucus   A thick, sticky liquid the body makes.

peak flow meter   A tool that measures how well the airways are working.

pollen   A fine, powdery dust made by flowers and trees.

triggers   Things that set off an asthma attack.

wheeze   To breathe with difficulty, often with a whistling sound.

Read More

Borgert-Spaniol, Megan. **All about Asthma.** Inside Your Body. Minneapolis: Super Sandcastle, 2019.

Kawa, Katie. **What Happens When Someone Has Asthma?** The KidHaven Health Library. New York: KidHaven Publishing, 2020.

Smith, Ryan. **Asthma.** In Case of Emergency. New York: AV2, 2021.

Websites

KIDSHEALTH: ASTHMA

https://kidshealth.org/en/kids/asthma.html

Read this website to learn more about asthma.

PBS KIDS: ARTHUR FAMILY HEALTH: ASTHMA

https://pbskids.org/arthur/health/asthma

Find helpful information about asthma.

WONDEROPOLIS: WHAT CAUSES ASTHMA ATTACKS?

https://wonderopolis.org/wonder/what-causes-asthma-attacks

Learn more about asthma from this education site.

Every effort has been made to ensure that these websites are appropriate for children. However, because of the nature of the Internet, it is impossible to guarantee that these sites will remain active indefinitely or that their contents will not be altered.